Original title:
A World in Frost

Copyright © 2024 Swan Charm
All rights reserved.

Author: Paulina Pähkel
ISBN HARDBACK: 978-9916-79-411-1
ISBN PAPERBACK: 978-9916-79-412-8
ISBN EBOOK: 978-9916-79-413-5

The Dance of Crystal Light

In a world where shadows play,
Crystal beams weave night and day.
Colors twirl, a gentle sway,
Nature's art in grand display.

Glittering drops from leaves above,
Radiate warmth like whispering love.
Dreams take flight on wings of dove,
As starlit skies our hearts speak of.

In the silent forest deep,
Moonlight's glow, a secret keep.
While the tired night-time weep,
The crystal dance begins to leap.

Each petal shines with morning dew,
Awakening life, a vibrant hue.
In the mist, the world feels new,
A tapestry of all that's true.

As dawn approaches, shadows fade,
Yet in memories, the dance cascades.
The crystal light, in magic made,
Lives on in hearts that have portrayed.

Serenity in Frosted Shadows

Amidst the frost, a silence grows,
Whispers soft like winter snows.
Nature wraps in gentle prose,
In tranquil dance, the beauty flows.

Underneath the silver sky,
Where feathered flakes like dreams do lie.
Restful thoughts, they softly sigh,
In a world where worries die.

Trees adorned in icy lace,
Offer solace, a warm embrace.
In this stillness, find your place,
Breath of winter, soft and grace.

Footprints trace the silent ground,
In the calm, true peace is found.
Frosted shadows all around,
Echo light with gentle sound.

With each moment, time stands still,
Nature's pulse, a soothing thrill.
In the cold, our spirits fill,
With serenity, our hearts fulfill.

Icy Fingerprints of Time

In the depths of winter's chill,
Frozen whispers linger still,
Traces left on silvered snow,
Memories where shadows flow.

Frosty patterns grace the dawn,
In their silence, time is drawn,
Each delicate, pristine line,
Marks the moments that define.

Crystal edges, sharp and bright,
Capturing the fleeting light,
Footprints lost in endless white,
Where the day dissolves to night.

Echoes of the past remain,
In the frost, a soft refrain,
Icy fingerprints blend and fade,
Time's embrace, a gentle braid.

Winter's grasp holds all in sway,
Leading thoughts that drift away,
Yet within the freeze, we find,
Life's eternal, moving bind.

Boundless Stillness in a Shattered Glass

Fragments dance in light's embrace,
Shattered visions pulse and trace,
Every piece a story told,
Whispers delicate, yet bold.

Reflections of a fleeting dream,
Caught in chaos, yet they gleam,
Silent echoes fill the room,
Boundless stillness hides the gloom.

Colors blend in shards of fate,
Beauty born from loss, sedate,
In the stillness, hearts collide,
Finding solace where dreams bide.

Infinite in fractured ways,
Moments linger, softly gaze,
Through the breaks, the light streams in,
Promising what lies within.

Each sharp edge a tale you weave,
In the quiet, we believe,
That from chaos, peace will rise,
Boundless stillness never lies.

Dreams Adrift on Winter's Tide

Beneath the sky of silver gray,
Dreams are adrift, they spin and sway,
Carried on the frosty breeze,
Whispers riding through the trees.

Gentle snowflakes, soft and small,
Float like secrets, heed their call,
Winter's tide, a quiet sweep,
Cradling hopes in crystalline sleep.

Time suspends as moments blend,
In the stillness, thoughts ascend,
Dreams unspooled, soft and light,
Drifting further, out of sight.

Chasing shadows, lost in white,
Hearts entwined in this long night,
Embers glimmer, warmth remains,
Love's sweet echo in the chains.

As the dawn begins to break,
From the slumber, we awake,
Dreams once drifted, now arise,
Floating softly to the skies.

The Harmony of Frosted Whispers

In the quiet of the frost,
Gentle secrets, never lost,
Whispers wrap the world in lace,
Nature's sigh, a soft embrace.

Harmony in every flake,
Eager to the silence wake,
Frosted breaths of winter's song,
Carry sentiments along.

Leaves of ice on branches gleam,
Liquid silver, nature's dream,
Every crystal holds a tale,
Sentiments that never fail.

Voices carried on the wind,
Echo softly, where we've been,
In the hush, our hearts will meet,
Finding rhythm, pure and sweet.

Frosted whispers, chill and warm,
In their embrace, we transform,
With each breeze, the world shall know,
Harmony in winter's glow.

Dances of Frosty Mornings

In dawn's embrace, a chill descends,
Whispers of frost where daylight bends.
Soft swirls of white upon the trees,
Nature's canvas, a moment to seize.

Footprints linger on the glistening ground,
Silent echoes in this beauty found.
Each breath a cloud, a fleeting sigh,
As winter's spirit begins to fly.

The sun peeks through, a golden thread,
Weaving warmth where ice once spread.
A dance of light on frozen streams,
Awakening the world from dreams.

Hushed Footsteps on Crystal Streets

The world drapes in a silver glow,
With each soft step, the whispers flow.
Hushed echoes on the icy lane,
Crystal pathways filled with gain.

Street lamps flicker, casting light,
Guiding wanderers through the night.
Footfalls crunch in rhythmic ways,
Melodies of winter's praise.

Beneath the stars, a quiet song,
Where hearts beat soft, and souls belong.
Every step tells tales untold,
Of dreams woven in the cold.

The Poetry of Shimmering Silence

In the stillness, secrets bloom,
Soft murmurs break the chilly gloom.
Snowflakes dance with quiet grace,
Embracing Earth in their lace.

Silence holds a sacred space,
Where nature whispers, time drapes lace.
Each moment a verse, gently penned,
In an endless poem that will not end.

The moon casts shadows, silver bright,
Painting dreams in the velvet night.
With every breath, the world aligns,
In the poetry of shimmering signs.

Frosty Veins of the Earth

The ground beneath, a frosty shell,
Whispers tales it yearns to tell.
Veins of ice run deep and wide,
Holding warmth that the world can't hide.

Snow-capped hills, a tranquil crest,
Nature's heart beats in its rest.
With each pulse, life renews the land,
As seasons shift, a painter's hand.

Through cracks of frost, the earth will sigh,
Longing for spring, as days drift by.
In frozen veins, the life-threads flow,
Nurturing seeds yet to grow.

The Symphony of Frost and Shadows

In the quiet of the night,
Frost dances in the air,
Shadows stretching softly,
Invisible threads laid bare.

Stars glimmer like whispers,
Echoes in the dark,
Winter's breath, a secret,
A chill, a fleeting spark.

Trees adorned in diamonds,
Branches bow with grace,
Nature's soft serenade,
In this cold embrace.

The moon's luminous gaze,
Watches over all,
As frost weaves its magic,
And shadows start to fall.

In this symphony of silence,
The world holds its breath,
Each note a frozen memory,
Life awakens from death.

Melodies from the Frozen Canopy

Beneath a quilt of white,
The earth takes a pause,
Melodies gently rise,
In a frozen cause.

Whispers of the branches,
Singing to the sky,
Snowflakes swirl like dancers,
As time glides by.

The canopy above,
A crystal dome so bright,
Harmonies of winter,
Only felt at night.

Echoes of the valley,
Softly hum along,
The pulse of frozen tales,
In a winter song.

Each note, a gentle memory,
Of the warmth once there,
But now in ice encapsulated,
A harmony so rare.

Frostbitten Tales Under Silvered Skies

Under skies of silver,
Stories drift like snow,
Frostbitten whispers call,
From valleys down below.

Each flake a tale of yore,
Spun by winter's hand,
Echoes of the ancients,
In this frozen land.

Footprints in the powder,
Lead to paths unseen,
Tales of love and loss,
In the chilly sheen.

The moon, a silver beacon,
Illuminates the night,
Revealing hidden secrets,
In the pale moonlight.

With every step, a story,
Etched in frost so fine,
Beneath the silvered heavens,
Our hearts intertwine.

The Artistry of Winter's Canvas

Winter paints with grace,
A canvas dressed in white,
Every stroke, a whisper,
In the soft moonlight.

Branches dipped in silver,
Frost upon the ground,
Nature's artwork blooms,
In the silence found.

Colors fade to subtle,
As shadows blend and sway,
The artistry of stillness,
Marks the close of day.

As night moves in a dance,
The stars start to gleam,
A masterpiece of winter,
Drawn from a dream.

In this frozen gallery,
We find peace and calm,
Winter's art, a treasure,
Wrapped in nature's balm.

Serenade Beneath a Crystal Sky

Beneath the stars, we softly sway,
The moonlit glow guides our way.
Whispers of love in the night air,
Two hearts in rhythm, a perfect pair.

Gentle breezes carry our song,
Together in this space we belong.
Silver clouds drift like dreams above,
In this serenade, we find our love.

Notes that dance through the glowing dark,
Each melody ignites a spark.
Moments cherished, we hold them tight,
Under the serenade, we take flight.

Through velvet nights and dawn's first gleam,
We paint the world with every dream.
Hand in hand, in joy we tread,
In this crystal sky, our spirits wed.

As the night unfolds with grace,
We'll linger here in this embrace.
Together forever, with hearts so free,
Beneath a crystal sky, just you and me.

The Stillness Within the Chill

Winter wraps the world in white,
Softly muffling sound and light.
Trees stand silent, arms outspread,
In the stillness, time is led.

Snowflakes tumble slow and sure,
Each a wonder, soft and pure.
Breath hangs heavy in the air,
A quiet moment, still and rare.

Footsteps crunch on frost-kissed ground,
In this calm, peace can be found.
Nature's lull, a gentle sigh,
Underneath the muted sky.

Whispers of frost on windows lay,
Stories told in shades of gray.
In this chill, warmth gently grows,
Wrapped in stillness, love bestows.

As the dawn breaks, silent, slow,
Emerging light will softly show.
With every breath, we feel the thrill,
Embrace the stillness within the chill.

Exhalations of a Frosty Twilight

As daylight wanes, the sky turns blue,
A frosty breath that bids adieu.
Twilight whispers, soft and bright,
Embracing all in fading light.

Each exhalation, a cloud of white,
Hints of magic in the twilight.
Stars awaken, one by one,
As day retreats and night's begun.

A canvas painted with shades of gray,
Nature's art at the end of day.
In this moment, hearts align,
Lost in beauty, yours and mine.

The chill wraps round, a tender dress,
Cozy echoes, warmth to possess.
In this dusk, we find our peace,
As frosty twilight's wonders cease.

With every star that starts to glow,
We breathe in dreams, let worries go.
Together we'll savor this delight,
In the exhalations of the frost's twilight.

Snowbound Wishes on Lingering Breath

Blankets of white on the world below,
Every flake a wish we sow.
In the stillness, hopes take flight,
Snowbound dreams in the quiet night.

Frosty whispers swirl and dance,
Each moment gives us a chance.
With every breath, the magic flows,
In the snowbound hush, our love grows.

Captured moments, fleeting and rare,
Snowflakes twirl through the frosty air.
Every sigh, a wish we share,
Lingering warmth, beyond compare.

As dawn breaks through the morning mist,
We hold our dreams with a tender fist.
In this winter's glow, we believe,
Snowbound wishes, we shall achieve.

Under the sky of silvery hue,
In the heart, a promise true.
Together in snow, we take a breath,
Wishes linger, defying death.

Whispers of Winter's Breath

Whispers rise with the chill,
A dance upon the snow,
Softly fading like the light,
Of a day that bids adieu.

Branches bow beneath the weight,
Every flake a frozen gem,
Nature's quilt all draped in white,
A world asleep, held in mercy's hem.

Footsteps crunching on the path,
Echoes of a tranquil trance,
Silent secrets weave through trees,
Inviting hearts to take a chance.

Breath visible in the air,
Clouds of warmth on a cold night,
Voices soft like falling snow,
Binding souls with delight.

The moon spills silver on the ground,
While shadows stretch and play,
Stars awaken one by one,
A wondrous winter's ballet.

Crystal Veils of Silence

Crystal veils drape the earth,
Diamond hues of early morn,
Silent whispers in the air,
Magical, serene, reborn.

Each tree dons a frosty crown,
Patterns etched in softest light,
Nature's art is on display,
A canvas pure and white.

Every breath creates a cloud,
Fleeting dreams in bitter cold,
Winter's breath, a gentle sigh,
Stories waiting to be told.

In this stillness, echoes ring,
Of laughter, love, and hope anew,
Captured in the tranquil light,
The world feels fresh and true.

As shadows lengthen, gold descends,
A tapestry of dusk and dawn,
In crystal veils, we find our peace,
As winter's spell lingers on.

Glacial Dreams at Dawn

Glacial dreams at break of day,
Awakening the frozen land,
Softly painted by the sun,
With a gentle, warming hand.

The horizon blushes bright,
Colors dance in morning's light,
Whispers of a new beginning,
Chasing shadows out of sight.

Misty veils twirl in the breeze,
Echoing the night's serene,
Nature stirs from slumber deep,
Awaits the warmth, still pristine.

Crystalline lakes reflect the sky,
Mirrors of a world so still,
In their depths, the dreams reside,
Boundless, endless, and fulfilled.

As dawn unfolds its tender grace,
Every heartbeat finds its place,
In glacial dreams, we seek and find,
A harmony that time won't erase.

Echoes in the Icebound Forest

Echoes call through the tall pines,
Carried on the wintry breeze,
Hidden voices softly weave,
Tales of time, ancient mysteries.

Frost encrusts the branches bare,
Each step forward crackles loud,
In this realm of whispered thoughts,
The snow forms a gentle shroud.

The heartbeats of a world asleep,
Resound through the quiet grove,
Nature's pulse beneath the frost,
Unveiling dreams we seldom know.

In the stillness, magic thrives,
Creating wonders yet unseen,
Where echoes blend with falling snow,
And shadows dance, serene and keen.

Time itself seems to suspend,
In this icebound land so vast,
Where echoes linger, memories blend,
And the beauty of winter holds fast.

Frosty Whispers from the Quiet Glen

In the hush of the glen, frost does cling,
Whispers of silence, a soft offering.
Branches adorned in a crystal lace,
Nature holds breath in this tranquil space.

Moonlight dances on the frozen stream,
Echoes of night weave a wintry dream.
Stars twinkle softly in the darkened eaves,
Clothed in the quiet, the forest believes.

Shadows slide gently on snow-covered ground,
Echoes of life in the stillness are found.
Footprints like secrets tell tales of the past,
Moments of magic adorned with a cast.

Frost-kissed whispers float through the air,
Every cold breath, a sign of care.
Beneath the blanket where soft silence dwells,
The heartbeat of winter, a story it tells.

As dawn breaks gently, colors unfold,
A tapestry woven with threads of gold.
Frosty whispers in the quiet glen,
Nature's embrace welcomes us again.

The Radiance of Chilled Stars

Chilled stars above, in the evening sky,
Glimmers of hope where the shadows lie.
Each point of light, a frozen breath,
Twinkling softly in a dance with death.

Radiant hues from a world afar,
Whispering secrets of each shining star.
The cosmos cradles the chill of night,
Painting the darkness with celestial light.

The night air sparkles, crisp and clear,
Echoing dreams that linger near.
Every heartbeat aligns with the spheres,
Embracing the stillness that erases fears.

In the quiet moments, the soul takes flight,
Guided by the radiance of chilled light.
Wrapped in the velvet of endless sky,
Hopes and wishes through starlit sighs.

From frozen realms to the heart below,
The universe shares the secrets we sow.
In the embrace of night, dreams ignite,
The radiance of chilled stars shines so bright.

Glimmering Paths of Frozen Twilight

Twilight descends with a gentle glow,
Paths of ice shimmer where soft winds blow.
Footsteps glide over the silken white,
Tracing the warmth that fades into night.

Glimmering visions beckon, unfold,
Stories of winter in whispers told.
Each path reflects memories held dear,
Echoing laughter, a flicker of cheer.

In the heart of twilight, shadows blend,
Glimmers of hope that never quite end.
Every step forward, a silent vow,
To cherish the magic of frozen now.

As stars awaken, the night takes hold,
Glistening dreams like dust made of gold.
Glimmering paths weave through time and space,
In the twilight's embrace, we find our place.

Through frozen echoes and shimmering light,
We wander, we ponder, in the cool night.
With every heartbeat, we carve our way,
On glimmering paths where shadows play.

The Art of Perpetual Winter

In a world wrapped in frost's gentle sway,
Winter unveils its artistic display.
Every flake falls like a whispered thought,
Crafting a masterpiece, nature's own art.

Snowflakes linger on branches and leaves,
Painting a portrait that softly deceives.
Each icy crystal a story untold,
Echoing beauty in silver and gold.

The chill in the air sings songs of the cold,
Shimmering secrets in the silence unfold.
A canvas of white, limitless and vast,
In the art of winter, memories last.

Under the moon's watchful gaze tonight,
Every shadow dances, a calm, pure light.
Nature's hand brushes the world with grace,
Creating wonders in this sacred space.

Embrace the magic wrapped in a chill,
For winter's sweet whispers are all that fulfill.
The art of perpetual winter shall soar,
A symphony frozen that forever endures.

Whispers of Winter's Veil

Snowflakes dance in the frozen air,
Whispers soft, a secret shared.
Beneath the quilt of silent white,
Dreams are woven in the night.

Trees stand tall in frosty grace,
Branches framed, a crystal lace.
Stars twinkle in the deep dark skies,
Telling tales of winter sighs.

Footsteps trace a silent path,
Crunching softly in winter's math.
The world dressed in purest white,
Holds its breath in the still night.

Icicles hanging, sharp and bright,
Glistening in the soft moonlight.
Each moment frozen, pure delight,
In winter's peaceful, serene sight.

The air is crisp, the heart feels bold,
In whispers felt, but never told.
Winter's veil cloaks all around,
In its embrace, tranquility found.

Shimmering Silence

In quietude the shadows play,
A shimmering glow at end of day.
Stars emerge in velvet skies,
Whispers float like gentle sighs.

The world asleep, a tranquil space,
Moonlight weaves a silver lace.
Night's embrace, a soothing balm,
In its arms, a tender calm.

Trees sway softly, a whispered tune,
Underneath a watching moon.
The heart drifts in peaceful grace,
Finding solace in this place.

Each star a dream, a wish held tight,
In shimmering silence, pure delight.
Moments linger, soft as air,
Wrapped in night, a love affair.

In stillness deep, where echoes fade,
Silhouettes in the twilight made.
Shimmering silence, a sweet refrain,
Woven softly through joy and pain.

Icy Embrace of Dawn

Morning breaks with icy breath,
A tender touch, a dance with death.
Frosted fields in pastel hues,
Bathed in light, the earth renews.

Birds awaken, sing their song,
Filling silence, where dreams belong.
The sun ascends, a golden ray,
Chasing the shadows of the gray.

Stillness cloaks the waking world,
As icy tendrils gently unfurled.
Nature stirs in vibrant threads,
Weaving warmth where silence treads.

Breath of frost, a fleeting kiss,
In the dawn, a moment's bliss.
With every ray, the night gives way,
To a bright promise of the day.

In icy grasp, yet warmth abounds,
With every heartbeat, life resounds.
Dawn unfolds its tender dream,
In the embrace of sunlight's gleam.

Crystal Dreams in the Twilight

Twilight whispers, colors blend,
Softly fading as day does end.
Crimson skies meet indigo,
In crystal dreams, where shadows grow.

The horizon hums a gentle tune,
Bathed in the light of the rising moon.
Stars peek out through veils of night,
Casting wishes in fading light.

Reflections dance on silver streams,
Carrying softly our dreams.
Each breath comes slow, the world at ease,
In twilight's arms, our spirits tease.

A tapestry of dusk unfurled,
Kissed by magic, it holds the world.
Every moment, a fleeting gleam,
In the heart of twilight's dream.

As night descends, the calm prevails,
Beneath the sky, our story sails.
In crystal dreams, we find our way,
Guided softly to the end of day.

The Chime of Glacial Joy

In the still of winter's breath,
A soft echo hangs so clear,
Chimes of ice in quiet depth,
Whisper secrets we hold dear.

Fractured light in crystal waves,
Gliding through the frosty air,
Nature sings of joyful graves,
Beneath the weight of snow so fair.

Frozen laughter fills the space,
Chilled yet warming to the core,
Every flake finds its own place,
Dancing down forevermore.

Hope is wrapped in winter's gleam,
Softly twinkling, pure and bright,
In this world, we dream our dream,
United by the silver light.

With each chime, a story told,
Of resilience in the cold,
In glacial joy, our hearts unfold,
Embracing warmth, the future bold.

Frozen Lattice of Forgotten Time

Beneath the snow, the past resides,
A tapestry of fleeting threads,
In silence, ancient wisdom hides,
A lattice where the frost now spreads.

Memories etched in icy lace,
Fractured moments held in trance,
Time dances softly, leaves no trace,
Yet calls us forth to take a chance.

Each pattern sings of things unknown,
A world of whispers buried deep,
In twilight's grip, they softly moan,
Awakening dreams from their sleep.

The frozen beauty tells a tale,
Of lives once lived, now wrapped in chill,
In every crystal, dreams prevail,
A haunting grace, a tranquil thrill.

Through thawing frost, the past may breathe,
And memories begin to thaw,
With every step, we take and weave,
A path to futures we might draw.

An Enigma Wrapped in Snow

In winter's grip, a secret sleeps,
Beneath the veil of white so pure,
An enigma that softly keeps,
Mysteries we yearn to cure.

A hush possesses all around,
As snowflakes fall in gentle swirl,
Each one a thought that can be found,
In layers deep, where whispers twirl.

At dusk, the shadows weave and blend,
Creating stories yet untold,
Echoes of hearts that twist and bend,
Wrapped in frost like breath of gold.

Footprints lost in quiet dreams,
The path obscured by winter's sigh,
Yet hope glimmers, softly beams,
Amidst the chill, we learn to fly.

An enigma kissed by the night,
In solitude, the truth ignites,
With every flake, we gain our sight,
Unraveling the frozen heights.

The Crystal-Studded Veil

A veil of crystals drapes the dawn,
Each facet gleaming, cold yet warm,
In winter's grasp, the world is drawn,
To beauty locked in nature's charm.

Softly glistening, a dreamlike shroud,
Draping trees in sparkling grace,
The morning sun peeks through the cloud,
Illuminating every place.

With every step, a crunching sound,
Echoes of winter's soft ballet,
Where magic lingers all around,
In the hush of this frozen play.

What stories hide beneath the frost?
The tales of life, of loss and gain,
In silent beauty, nothing lost,
As we embrace the frozen rain.

With each breath, the crystal glows,
A tapestry of light and shade,
In winter's hold, our wonder grows,
In every flake, a song is laid.

Chilled Echoes of Forgotten Melodies

In the stillness, whispers call,
A time once vibrant, now so small.
Notes linger like shadows of frost,
Echoes of beauty in silence lost.

Frozen hearts, they sway in trance,
Memories dance in a fleeting chance.
Through winds that howl, a soft refrain,
Lost in the ether, the joy, the pain.

Shattered strings of a distant sound,
With each breath, shadows gather 'round.
Waves of chill on the breath of night,
Haunted by dreams, they take their flight.

Crystalline echoes weave the air,
Fragments of laughter, buried with care.
Songs of old in the twilight gleam,
Softly they fade, like a soft dream.

In shivering dusk, the notes drift free,
Carried on winds, a delicate plea.
Through chill and silence, they find their way,
In echoes of winter, forever they'll stay.

Songs of the Icy Horizon

On the brink where the blue meets gray,
Silent whispers beckon and sway.
Beyond the edge, where the cold winds sigh,
Harmonies linger in the vast, deep sky.

A frosted tune beneath a pale sun,
Every note is a story begun.
Winds carry tales from shores unknown,
Songs of the icy, the lost, the lone.

In the distance, a melody calls,
Resonant depths where the nightfall falls.
With every breath of the biting chill,
Echoes of longing are haunting still.

Snowflakes scatter like whispered keys,
Unlocking secrets in the frozen breeze.
Inbound harmonies, brisk and bright,
Sing of the dawn in the heart of night.

From the horizon where silence reigns,
Spring forth the songs that break the chains.
In frigid beauty, the voices soar,
Melodies linger and forever explore.

Vestiges of Light in a Frozen World

Amidst the frost, a flicker shines,
Glimmers of hope on thin, weak lines.
In a world draped in icy despair,
Vestiges of light linger in the air.

Candles glow against the deep, dark sky,
Their warmth abandoned, yet they try.
Shadows stretch as the night unfolds,
Stories untold in the cold wind's hold.

In the realm where silence weaves,
Echoes of laughter sway with leaves.
With each small spark, the shadows play,
Chasing the darkness, they fade away.

Crystals catching the softest gleam,
Reflecting dreams in a muted stream.
In the stillness, whispers of cheer,
Light dances gently for those who hear.

In the frozen breath of the waiting night,
Hope thrives softly, a resilient light.
From the abyss, where shadows swirl,
Rise the vestiges in a frozen world.

Routed Paths Through Shrouded Snow

Beneath the drift, old paths are laid,
Carved by footsteps where dreams once played.
Shrouded in white, the trails entwine,
Whispers of journeys, lost in time.

With every step, a muffled call,
The silent woods seem to enthrall.
Through vale and hill, the route grows thin,
Nature's embrace wraps softly within.

Endless echoes graze the air,
Footprints tell tales with a gentle flair.
From hollowed trees to the starry dome,
In the crisp night, the wandering roam.

Moonlit glimmers on frozen streams,
Carrying wishes born from dreams.
Paths converge in the wintry glow,
Stories linger where few may go.

Through shrouded snow, the heart finds peace,
With every turn, the burdens cease.
As dreams unfurl in the sacred night,
Routed paths blossom in soft moonlight.

The Fragile Art of Winter's Touch

The world dons a frosted gown,
Silent whispers, cold and brown.
Each flake dances from the sky,
A fleeting moment, whispering bye.

Bare branches wear a crystal sheen,
Nature's canvas, so serene.
Footprints tread on paths of white,
Captured magic in fading light.

A hush blankets the sleeping ground,
Winter's breath, a gentle sound.
Softly cradled, the earth waits,
In icy arms, it contemplates.

Stars peek through the velvet night,
Twinkling jewels, pure delight.
Beneath the moon's watchful gaze,
Time stands still in winter's haze.

Winter's touch, both fierce and mild,
In its grasp, the heart is wild.
Beauty found in every shard,
A fragile art that leaves us scarred.

Breath of the Icebound Hills

At dawn, the hills wear misty veils,
Echoing soft, the winter trails.
Silent shadows stretch and sigh,
Beneath the pale, expansive sky.

Frosted grass in silence grows,
The breath of winter, stillness flows.
Crisp air bites, but hearts stay warm,
Wrapped in layers, safe from harm.

Every ridge cloaked in white lace,
Nature's wonder, a quiet grace.
The world feels hushed, as time slows down,
In this frosty, sleepless town.

Footsteps crunch on frozen ground,
In every sound, the peace is found.
Echoes linger in the chill,
Breath of the icebound, strong and still.

As twilight wraps the day's last light,
Stars awaken to join the night.
Embraced by cold, the hills confess,
In winter's arms, they find their rest.

Secrets Beneath the Snow's Embrace

Beneath the blanket, whispers dwell,
Stories woven, deep to tell.
Frozen secrets guard the ground,
In silent slumber, truth is found.

Crystal layers hide the past,
Moments captured, shadows cast.
Each flake carries a tale so old,
In winter's grip, the secrets hold.

Branches cradle the weight of white,
Nurtured thoughts in the night.
Every drift, a moment trapped,
In nature's quilt, all dreams are wrapped.

As spring approaches, warmth will bloom,
Yet winter holds the quiet gloom.
The heart remembers, though things move on,
Promises linger in the dawn.

In the silence, hope resides,
While soft snow mutes the world outside.
Beneath the white, life waits and sees,
Secrets whispered on the breeze.

Glimmers of Light on Frozen Ground

Sunrise spills its golden rays,
Painting hues on winter's glaze.
Glimmers dance on icy streams,
Life awakens, stirs our dreams.

Footprints mark the crystal trails,
As laughter echoes, joy prevails.
Nature wakes in colors bright,
Chasing shadows, welcoming light.

Silent flurries gently fall,
Enveloping the world in thrall.
Each glimmer holds a story's spark,
Illuminating memories' mark.

Frosty breath, a fleeting gaze,
At twilight's edge, the daylight fades.
In every glimmer, life's embrace,
Frozen ground hides warmth and grace.

Stars return to paint the night,
Wistful wishes take their flight.
In every icy, glistening crown,
Hope is reborn on frozen ground.

Frost's Embrace in Dusk's Glow

In twilight's hush, the frost descends,
A shimmering veil that gently bends.
Whispers of cold in the evening's breath,
Hold secrets deep, as day meets death.

Trees adorned in crystalline lace,
Each branch a mirror, a still embrace.
Dusk's glow dances on frozen streams,
As night unfolds its starry dreams.

Misty shadows cloak the land,
Nature's artwork, calm and grand.
Beneath the sky's soft, fading light,
Frosty kisses greet the night.

In this serene, enchanted sight,
Frost cradles warmth in a gentle bite.
The world a canvas, pure and bright,
Endless beauty, pure delight.

The Solitude of Icebound Journeys

In silent lands where no bird sings,
The icebound journeys hold strange things.
Footprints linger on a frozen path,
Echoes of laughter in nature's wrath.

Mountains loom like ancient kings,
Guardians of time, and whispering springs.
Each icy breath brings tales to tell,
Of solitude where spirits dwell.

A barren lake reflects the sky,
Where dreams take flight, yet dared to die.
The chill of night wraps all in lace,
As shadows dance in empty space.

Each journey marked by the frost's embrace,
Reminds us of nature's fleeting grace.
In solitude, we find our way,
A path of quiet in the fray.

Threads of Time in a Frozen Landscape

Woven tightly in winter's grip,
Time stands still, a whispered slip.
Frosty threads of ages past,
Each moment stitched, yet none can last.

The landscape, timeless, vast, and white,
Where shadows fade into the night.
Trees hold stories in their bark,
As ice blankets all, hushed and stark.

Sunrise paints the world anew,
Gold and silver blend in view.
Moments twinkle like frosty stars,
In a land untouched by scars.

Frozen echoes softly call,
In the serenity, we find it all.
Each thread of time, a fleeting ghost,
In the stillness, we love the most.

Beneath the Layers of Ice

Beneath the ice, life waits in dreams,
Hidden deep within silent streams.
Layers thick, yet fragile too,
Whispers of green where the cold is blue.

Silent rhythms beneath the frost,
Revelations of life, never lost.
Each breath of wind, a tale untold,
Of warmth and life, beneath the cold.

The stillness holds a gentle grace,
While nature composes its slowed embrace.
In the quiet, secrets murmur soft,
Beneath the layers, life drifts aloft.

Awake the spirit from winter's hold,
In silent chambers, stories unfold.
Nature's strength, a tender fight,
Beneath the ice, awaits the light.

Unveiling the Secrets of Frosted Dawn

Whispers of dawn in silver light,
Frosted petals, pure and bright.
Nature holds its breath so deep,
Secrets wrapped in winter's sleep.

Glistening trees, a silent choir,
Icicles hang like chains of fire.
Footprints crunch on winter's breath,
Marking paths of life and death.

A soft glow breaks through the haze,
Painting shadows with sun's rays.
Each glance reveals a hidden spark,
A canvas born from night's cold dark.

Layers of frost tell tales untold,
Stories of warmth in winter's fold.
Eager sparks of life awake,
As daylight breaks the icy lake.

Mysteries etched in cold embrace,
Nature's work, a timeless grace.
In the chill, we hear the call,
The secrets shared with one and all.

Frosty Echoes in Twilight's Grasp

Echoes shimmer in the night,
Frosty whispers take to flight.
Twilight casts a gentle spell,
In the silence, secrets dwell.

Stars ignite a frozen sky,
Dancing gently, oh so high.
Each breath visible, a fleeting sigh,
As the world begins to lie.

Moonlit paths of crystal white,
Guiding dreams that take their flight.
In this hush, heartbeats draw near,
As winter's magic begins to steer.

Frosty echoes softly chime,
In the tapestry of time.
Nature's voice sings low and clear,
In this stillness, nothing to fear.

Weaving tales of ancient lore,
In the twilight, we explore.
Every shadow holds a truth,
As frost unlocks the gift of youth.

The Ethereal Dance of Winter's Muse

Winter's muse in graceful sway,
Spins a tale in soft array.
Lace of snowflakes, pure and fine,
In her arms, the world aligns.

Dancing lightly, she will glide,
Through the whispers, side by side.
Stars outshine the evening's hush,
In the night where shadows blush.

Each flutter brings the night alive,
In her magic, spirits thrive.
Breath of frost in every turn,
Awakens hearts, a fierce yearn.

Through the drifts, her laughter sings,
Carrying warmth on frozen wings.
In her hold, the cold will fade,
As anew, the dawn is made.

Frozen dreams in twilight's glow,
Winter's muse, we long to know.
Ethereal songs paint the sky,
In the depths, we learn to fly.

A Tapestry of Ice and Light

A tapestry of ice unfolds,
Stitched with whispers, tales retold.
Every shard a story bright,
Woven gently into night.

Glacial rivers, pure delight,
Reflecting visions, soft and white.
Crystals dance in winter's hold,
Mirroring life in threads of gold.

Patterns twinkle in the haze,
A brilliant show through frosty maze.
Each flicker, a heartbeat's song,
Binding souls where we belong.

In the chill, a warmth ignites,
Palette rich in darks and lights.
Nature's brush, so skilled and grand,
Crafts a world at her command.

As daybreak weaves the icy seams,
A symphony of frozen dreams.
In this quilt of light and air,
We find our way through winter's glare.

Glacial Secrets in the Evening

Whispers weave through silent air,
A dance of ice without a care.
Shadows play on frozen stone,
In twilight's glow, the secrets grown.

Glistening hues of blue and white,
Embrace the chill, the fading light.
Each crystal spark ignites a dream,
As evening wraps its tranquil seam.

Beneath the stars, the glaciers sigh,
In frozen realms where echoes lie.
Time stands still in nature's hold,
A tale of beauty, silently told.

The mountains guard their pristine heart,
While evening paints with gentle art.
A world concealed in icy grace,
In shadows cast, a secret place.

Glacial breezes softly sweep,
Through ancient lands, their patience deep.
In every flake, a story flows,
Of lives once lived where silence grows.

Frigid Glimmers of Serenity

In morning's light, the frost does gleam,
A canvas crafted, pure and sweet.
Each breath, a cloud, a fleeting dream,
As nature bows, in stillness neat.

Rippling streams in icy chains,
Echoes of peace, soft refrains.
Glimmers dance on branches bare,
Frigid whispers fill the air.

The world cloaked in a crystal shroud,
Silent swirls of snow abound.
In wintry breath, the moments freeze,
A tranquil heart, a spirit's ease.

Beneath the sky of slate and gray,
The sun peeks through, a timid ray.
Each glimmer holds a promise still,
In frozen beauty, all is will.

With each soft step on frozen ground,
The world awakens, peace is found.
Frigid echoes, softest sighs,
In frosty veins, pure serenity lies.

The Frostbitten Path

A winding trail through crisp white fields,
Steps crunch softly, nature yields.
Each footprint tells of journeys bold,
A frosty tale of warmth untold.

Tall trees stand with coats of snow,
Guardians of paths where chill winds blow.
Branches arch like arms of grace,
Inviting all to this cold place.

Frostbite lingers on the skin,
But in the heart, a fire begins.
With steadfast hope, we push along,
The song of winter, our silent song.

In evening's grasp, the light will fade,
Yet shadows keep the dreams we made.
The frostbitten path leads us true,
With every step, a life anew.

Behind us lie the tales of old,
Paths of ice where hearts were bold.
In frigid air, we find our way,
To warmth and light, by break of day.

Slumbering Under a Powdered Sky

Beneath a quilt of snow so deep,
The world lies still, in gentle sleep.
Stars above weave tales of night,
In powdered skies so pure and bright.

Soft whispers float on winter's breath,
A hush that calms, it conquers death.
Every flake a whispered prayer,
Enveloping dreams in tender care.

The moon casts shadows, silver spun,
A lullaby when day is done.
Underneath the starry veil,
Nature breathes, a tranquil sail.

Each moment paused, a perfect bliss,
While time drifts on in frosty kiss.
Slumbering hearts in winter's light,
With powdered skies, the world feels right.

And as the dawn begins to rise,
Crimson blush of morning skies.
We wake anew, the shadows flee,
Underneath this magic, we are free.

Frosted Horizons of Longing

Beneath the veil of frosty light,
Hearts ache in the stillness of night.
Whispers carried on the chill,
Yearning thoughts that time can't still.

Moonlight dances on the snow,
In the silence, feelings grow.
Footsteps mark the paths we've crossed,
In this chill, we count the lost.

The world is wrapped in crystal dreams,
Yet hope lingers in quiet gleams.
With every breath, desires rise,
Beneath the vast and starry skies.

Branches bare, yet spirits high,
Frosted wishes float and fly.
A canvas white, untouched by hands,
In longing's grip, the heart still stands.

Eclipsed by shadows, we endure,
Through winters long, our souls are pure.
In frozen time, we seek the dawn,
Amidst the frost, we carry on.

The Icy Whisper of Hope

In the heart of winter's chill,
A soft whisper, serene and still.
Promises shimmer in the cold,
Stories of warmth, yet untold.

Frozen rivers, a gentle sigh,
Reflecting dreams that never die.
Hope, like ice, can bend and sway,
Guiding us through the longest day.

With every flake that falls from grace,
Nature's beauty starts to embrace.
The world wears white, a pure cocoon,
Beneath the light of a silver moon.

Echoes linger in the night,
The distant stars twinkle bright.
In quiet moments, we find our way,
The icy touch, a path to stay.

With hearts alight, we roam the frost,
Finding beauty in what's lost.
Through the silence, we hear our call,
The icy whisper, a love for all.

Dreams Encased in Silvery Threads

In the fabric of the night,
Dreams are woven, pure and bright.
Silvery threads of fleeting time,
Entwined in moments, soft as rhyme.

Stars like needles pierce the dark,
Stitching hopes with every spark.
Across the heavens, wishes soar,
Encased in threads, forevermore.

Through the stillness, they take flight,
Carried on the wings of night.
A tapestry of all we seek,
With every breath, our hearts grow weak.

Yet in the frost, we find our ground,
In winter's grasp, our dreams abound.
Encased in silver, pure and true,
We chase the light, where love breaks through.

With every dawn, new threads appear,
Binding us, drawing us near.
In frozen lands, our spirits tread,
Chasing dreams that lie ahead.

Withering Blossoms of Winter's Fury

In the grip of winter's breath,
Lies the tale of life and death.
Blossoms wither, beauty fades,
As icy winds steal sunlit glades.

Petals drift on frosty ground,
In silence, their whispers sound.
Memories of warmth, now lost,
Their vibrant hues, the bitter cost.

Yet in decay, a strength is found,
Resilience blooms in barren ground.
From withered stems, new life will spring,
In winter's hold, hope's echo sings.

The chill may bite, the chill may sting,
But through the frost, the heart can cling.
Emotions buried, yet they rise,
In dormant dreams, a new surprise.

So let the winter winds howl and roar,
As we endure, we long for more.
Withering blossoms pave the way,
For spring's embrace, a brighter day.

Traces of Light in a Glistening Abyss

In the depths where shadows dwell,
Flickers dance, a gentle spell.
Whispers of warmth in chilling night,
Traces of dreams, a glistening light.

Stars above, a cosmic sea,
Guiding lost souls, wild and free.
Each twinkle tells a tale so grand,
Of journeys taken, hand in hand.

Ripples spread on waters deep,
Silent secrets the abyss keeps.
Hope emerges from dark despair,
With traces of light, we find our care.

In the currents, we entwine,
Life's connections, pure, divine.
Through the chaos, we survive,
In the darkness, still we thrive.

Glistening paths we dare to tread,
With courage rising, fears shed.
Together we'll find our way through,
With traces of light, forever true.

The Silent Heartbeat of Ice

Beneath the hush of frozen night,
A rhythm beats, hidden from sight.
Crystals form in elegant grace,
The silent heartbeat, time's embrace.

Whispers travel through the chill,
Echoing dreams, a magic thrill.
Each crystalline shard a story untold,
Of seasons shifting, young and old.

In stillness, a world so alive,
Nature's pulse, a dance to survive.
As frost weaves blankets soft and white,
The silent heartbeat shines so bright.

Winds carry secrets through the trees,
Carving tales in the icy breeze.
Though cold may reign in endless nights,
The heart beats on, igniting lights.

In frozen realms of beauty rare,
We find the warmth of loving care.
For every heartbeat, a promise lies,
In the silent pulse, the spirit flies.

Reflections in the Frosty Expanse

Endless white, the world in trance,
Mirrored skies in a frozen dance.
Each step taken leaves its trace,
Reflections bloom in nature's grace.

Glistening fields, where dreams collide,
Silent whispers in the frost abide.
Footprints fading with the dawn,
Stories linger, though they're gone.

Beneath the surface, life awaits,
Captured in time, the heart sedates.
In icy depths, the echoes ring,
Reflections of what warmth can bring.

Frosted mirrors, we gaze anew,
In the vastness, souls break through.
Each frozen breath, a silent shout,
In this expanse, we dance about.

As twilight falls, the stars ignite,
Painting stories in the night.
The frosty expanse holds its breath,
In quiet beauty, it conquers death.

Lament of the Frostbitten Leaves

Once vibrant hues, now dulled and grey,
Frostbitten leaves, they drift away.
Whispers of autumn's fading breath,
In the cold, they mourn their death.

Each leaf a memory, rich, profound,
Now whispering softly, without a sound.
Fragile echoes of life's embrace,
Resting gently in winter's grace.

A tapestry wrought in chill and fear,
Nature weeps, yet we hold dear.
The cycle turns, with beauty found,
In the loss that wraps around.

Through barren branches, stories weave,
Of seasons gone and hearts that grieve.
In frost's hold, a tender plea,
For rebirth, for life, to set them free.

Yet even in the frost's cruel kiss,
There lies a promise, a hidden bliss.
For in lament, new life will sprout,
From frostbitten leaves, hope will shout.

Echoes of Stillness in a Grayed Horizon

In the quiet morn, shadows blend,
Whispers of dreams that seem to suspend.
Silence drapes the world, softly bright,
Where time stands still, lost in the light.

A cold breeze weaves through barren trees,
Echoes of memories dance with the leaves.
Each breath a ghost, a piece of the past,
In this gray expanse, moments hold fast.

Stillness takes root, feelings unfold,
Stories of warmth wrapped in the cold.
The horizon stretches, a canvas of gray,
Where echoes of silence guide the way.

Through fog's gentle touch, secrets reveal,
Nature's soft heartbeat, a pulse we feel.
In twilight's embrace, shadows softly play,
A symphony written in shades of the day.

As day meets night, sky begins to fade,
The echoes of stillness softly invade.
Each heartbeat whispers, a tale of its own,
In this grayed horizon, we're never alone.

The Enchantment of a Snow-draped Dream

Amidst the whispers of falling snow,
A blanket of silence begins to grow.
Each flake a dancer, graceful and light,
Weaving a tapestry, dazzling and white.

The moontip glimmers on the icy ground,
In this dreamscape, wonders abound.
Footsteps muffled, as if time stood still,
Wrapped in enchantment, hearts gently thrill.

Frosted windows frame a world so pure,
Magic in stillness, an age-old allure.
Each breath is a cloud, soft whispers ignite,
As dreams in the snow blend with the night.

A snow-draped vision, serene and divine,
Nature's artwork, a seamless design.
Each moment a treasure, a fleeting glance,
To be lost in the wonder, a silent dance.

With dawn's first light, colors softly gleam,
Awakening softly from a snow-draped dream.
Enchantment lingers where shadows retreat,
In the magic of winter, our hearts find their beat.

Winter's Lament in Frosty Hues

Amidst the chill of a frost-laden air,
Winter unravels a tale of despair.
Branches shiver in the biting wind's song,
Echoes of sorrow where we all belong.

The sky, a canvas of muted gray,
Hides sunlit colors, fading away.
Each snowflake falls, a tear from the sky,
In winter's lament, we sigh and comply.

Fields once vibrant, now blanketed white,
Whispers of laughter fade into the night.
Memories linger in shadows that creep,
While hearts yearn for warmth, in silence they weep.

Yet in this stillness, hope starts to bloom,
As frost-kissed dawn chases shadows of gloom.
With every breath, the promise of spring,
In winter's lament, new songs we will sing.

So let the cold wrap us tight in its hold,
For from these dark moments, we gather our gold.
In winter's embrace, lessons we learn,
That from the frostbite, new warmth will return.

Silhouettes Amidst Frosted Shadows

As day fades softly into a twilight glow,
Silhouettes emerge, dancing in the snow.
Frosted whispers weave tales in the night,
Where moments linger, lost in the light.

Shadows stretch long, a soft, silent dance,
In the chill of winter, dreams take their chance.
Bare trees stand watch, guardians of time,
Amidst frosted shadows, beauty in rhyme.

Each footstep crunches, a story unfolds,
In the quietest moments, the heart feels bold.
Shapes of the past, like whispers, they sway,
Silhouettes amidst frost, where memories play.

Under the stars, the world seems to pause,
Wrapped in the silence, we find our cause.
In these frosted shadows, life feels complete,
Each silhouette tells us that we're unique.

Together we wander, hand in hand we roam,
In the magic of winter, we find our home.
A canvas of shadows, shimmering bright,
Silhouettes of longing that dance in the night.

Chilling Echoes of the Past

Whispers dance in the cold air,
Memories linger everywhere.
Frosted windows tell their tale,
Haunting shadows softly wail.

In the stillness, voices hum,
Secrets held, time's quiet drum.
Voices lost but never fade,
In these echoes, truth is laid.

The world outside is dressed in white,
Silent whispers take to flight.
Every flake a story spun,
In the chill, all past is won.

Glimmers of a distant fire,
Filling hearts, igniting desire.
Footsteps fade, yet still they roam,
Chilling echoes bring us home.

Through the fog, we seek the light,
Guided by the stars so bright.
With each breath, we feel the pain,
Chilling echoes will remain.

Frosted Petals on Silent Ground

Petals fall on winter's breath,
Blankets soft, a shroud of death.
Whispers of the fading blooms,
Nature weeps in quiet rooms.

Each soft touch of ice and snow,
Cradles life as it must go.
Silent beauty, frozen grace,
In this stillness, time we trace.

Underneath the frosted veil,
Lives the hope that will prevail.
The ground sleeps, yet dreams of spring,
Waiting for the warmth to bring.

Trees stand bare, their whispers light,
Guarding secrets of the night.
Frosted petals on the way,
Mark the end of another day.

In the quiet, peace does reign,
Frosted petals hide the pain.
Time will turn with gentle sound,
Life returns to silent ground.

Hushed Breath of Winter

In the hush, the world is still,
Winter deepens with its thrill.
Frosted breath on every face,
Nature's calm, a soft embrace.

Snowflakes drift like whispered dreams,
Beneath the moon, the twilight gleams.
Branches bow with icy weight,
Time stands still; we contemplate.

Through the cold, the stars align,
Guiding hearts with light divine.
In this moment, silence reigns,
Hushed breath speaks where hope remains.

Voices low, a gentle tune,
Sung beneath the watching moon.
Every note, a sacred thread,
In the stillness, words are said.

Winter's heart holds stories dear,
In the quiet, crystal clear.
Feel the breath of time unwind,
Hushed whispers bind us, intertwined.

Fragments of a Glacial Heart

In the depths of ice and snow,
Lies a heart that beats so slow.
Shattered dreams like glassy shards,
Hiding truth behind cold guards.

Each fragment tells a silent tale,
Of love lost in the winter's gale.
Bitter frost, yet warm inside,
Longing for a place to hide.

Echoes whisper through the night,
Caught between the dark and light.
Flickers of a life once bright,
Beneath the stars, a heart takes flight.

Shards like diamonds dancing bright,
In the moon's embrace, pure delight.
Fragments lost but never gone,
Glacial heart beats on and on.

With each pulse, a story grows,
In the cold, true warmth still glows.
Gathered pieces, sharp and sweet,
Fragments of a heart, complete.

Driftwood Memories in Winter

Bare branches reach for gray skies,
Whispers of warmth in the cold air.
Footprints blur as the wind sighs,
Driftwood dreams, scattered and rare.

Frozen shores hold secrets tight,
Each wave a story left untold.
The sun sets early, a fleeting light,
Memories wrapped in the winter's fold.

Time pauses in this icy embrace,
Remnants of summers long gone by.
Nature's beauty in a tranquil space,
Driftwood carries tales of the sky.

In the stillness, hearts will find,
The echoes of laughter, soft and sweet.
Winter's breath in our minds entwined,
Driftwood memories beneath our feet.

So let the chill of this season stay,
Each moment cherished, held so dear.
In driftwood thoughts, we drift away,
Finding warmth in the cold's frontier.

A Ballet of Frost-Kissed Souls

In the moonlight, shadows twirl,
Frost-kissed souls take to the stage.
Nature's breath begins to swirl,
A dance of time, each heart a page.

Crystals glisten in the night,
An audience of stars above.
Each movement pure, graceful flight,
Embracing all with tender love.

Spirits rise as the night unfolds,
Bound by melodies soft and bright.
Whispers of winter, tales retold,
In the silence, they find their light.

The world transforms with every leap,
As frost weaves stories through the air.
A ballet played in shadows deep,
Each step crafted with utmost care.

In this moment, time stands still,
Frost-kissed souls unite as one.
A perfect harmony, a thrill,
As dawn approaches, the dance is done.

Hidden Crystal Gardens

Beneath the snow, a secret lies,
Crystal gardens in slumber deep.
Frozen flowers, a sweet surprise,
Nature's artwork, dreams to keep.

Glistening petals catch the light,
Diamonds scattered upon the ground.
In winter's chill, a pure delight,
Hidden beauty in silence found.

Each step reveals a sparkling trail,
Whispers of spring beneath the frost.
Time will come when colors prevail,
But for now, these treasures are lost.

Nature's canvas, white and serene,
A moment frozen, still, and pure.
In the silence, magic is seen,
Hidden gardens that will endure.

So let us wander, hand in hand,
Through this winter wonderland.
In hidden crystal gardens, we stand,
Awaiting blooms, soft and grand.

Echoes of Snow Beneath the Stars

Under a sky of twinkling light,
Echoes of snow softly call.
Footsteps quiet in the night,
Wrapped in peace, we feel it all.

Every flake an artist's touch,
Blanketing the world in white.
Each breath a moment, pure as such,
Lost in dreams, we drift from sight.

The night whispers secrets untold,
Every star a guardian bright.
In the silence, we grow bold,
Embracing the magic of the night.

Around us, shadows lightly dance,
As winter weaves its silent song.
In the stillness, we take a chance,
Finding where our hearts belong.

So let the echoes guide our way,
Through the snow and starlit skies.
In this moment, forever stay,
As the world sleeps and softly sighs.

The Stillness Between Seasons

In twilight's hush, the air is thick,
A pause between the tick and tock.
The trees stand bare, their branches sleek,
While whispers dance around the clock.

The ground is cloaked in muted tones,
Each step a breath, a memory.
The world awaits, no vibrant moans,
Just stillness in its reverie.

As evening falls, the shadows creep,
The sun bows low, its warmth will fade.
In silence deep, the earth will sleep,
And dreams of spring begin to wade.

A fleeting glance at life to come,
Buds nestled close beneath the crust.
In peacefulness, a quiet hum,
Of time that ebbs, yet we trust.

So linger here where moments blend,
In this embrace of soft decay.
The stillness whispers, "All things end,
But find your light within the gray."

Beneath the Frosted Canopy

A lace of frost on every limb,
Nature's quilt, so pure and white.
Beneath the trees, the echoes dim,
Holding secrets of the night.

With every breath, the cold bites deep,
Yet beauty rests within the chill.
A silent world, so vast, so steep,
In each still moment, hearts are still.

The canopy, a crystal dome,
Each droplet glints like starlit skies.
In this embrace, we find our home,
A sanctuary where hope lies.

As sunlight pierces through the frost,
The world awakens, soft and slow.
No warmth is lost, nor love is tossed,
Beneath the canopy, aglow.

So tread with care on glimmered ground,
With every step, a gentle grace.
Beneath the frost, life's pulse is found,
In nature's still and lovely space.

Lullabies of a Frozen Dawn

In morning's hush, the world unfolds,
A blanket thick with winter's breath.
The stories of the night retold,
In whispers soft, a sweet bequeath.

The sun creeps in, a tender light,
Melting dreams of icy shards.
Each radiance, a gentle fight,
Bestows the earth with warming guards.

The trees sway lightly, dressed in white,
Their branches bowed like solemn vows.
In chorus, nature greets the light,
And lifts its voice as life allows.

The air is filled with songs of time,
A lullaby that holds us fast.
With each soft note, we start to climb,
Through dreams of winter, shadows cast.

So listen close to dawn's embrace,
Where every sound can heal the heart.
In frozen hush, we find our place,
As lullabies of spring impart.

Glistening Veil of Light

A veil of light on morning's edge,
Transforms the world to purest gold.
With every dawn, we make a pledge,
To seek the warmth within the cold.

The crystals spark on blades of grass,
A glimmering song of nature's art.
As dew drops fall, this moment's pass,
We feel the rhythm of the heart.

Above, the sky, a canvas wide,
With hues of pink and gentle blue.
Each sunrise brings a swell of pride,
A brand new day, a chance anew.

The shadows stretch, then fade away,
A glistening promise in the air.
In light's embrace, we find our way,
Through every trial, every prayer.

So cherish this bright, fleeting sight,
For in its glow, our spirits soar.
In this embrace of purest light,
We find the strength to hope for more.

The Elegance of a Winter's Breath

Whispers on the frosty air,
Gentle sighs that dance and flare.
Each flake a delicate guise,
Painting dreams in the pale skies.

Trees draped in a shimmering veil,
Silent stories they unveil.
Footprints imprint on the white,
Memories fade with the light.

Time slows in the crystal glow,
Nature's pause in silent show.
Breezes hum a soft refrain,
Echoes of winter's sweet domain.

In a hush, the world lies still,
Chill and warmth, a subtle thrill.
A moment caught in snowy grace,
The heart finds its peaceful place.

As dusk wraps the day in dreams,
Moonlight casts its silver beams.
Winter breathes a soothing song,
With elegance, we all belong.

Serenade of the Icebound Night

Stars emerge in the evening sky,
While icy winds begin to sigh.
A serenade of silent night,
Wrapped in moon's gentle light.

Branches creak with whispered tales,
As shadows dance in the gales.
Each breath a puff of misty air,
Nature's secrets laid bare.

Frosted dreams begin to gleam,
In a world like a frozen dream.
Night blankets the earth in peace,
While silvered moments never cease.

Crickets cease their evening song,
In winter's arms where we belong.
The stillness deepens, time suspends,
In the night where magic transcends.

A lullaby of winter's grace,
Holds the heart in its embrace.
Serenade of icy delight,
In the calm of an enchanting night.

Solitude Wrapped in Ice Lace

Winter drapes the world in white,
A delicate lace that feels so right.
Solitude whispers in the snow,
Quiet places where the heart can grow.

Nature rests in her frozen gown,
Silence reigns in this sleepy town.
Fingers trace the windowpane,
Crystal patterns like a chain.

A moment held in tranquil air,
Life slows down without a care.
The chilly breath of winter's song,
Invites us to linger long.

Footsteps crunch on the powdered ground,
In solitude, peace is found.
Each silence holds a sacred space,
Wrapped in winter's gentle embrace.

As the sun dips behind the trees,
The evening frosts begin to tease.
Solitude wrapped in frost and grace,
In this winter's warm embrace.

Luminous Frost on Slumbering Fields

Morning wakes with a crystal sheen,
Fields aglow in frosty green.
Luminous frost twinkles bright,
Painting a scene of pure delight.

Sunrise kisses the icy ground,
Whispers of magic all around.
Nature sparkles, a wondrous show,
As the day begins to glow.

In stillness, beauty takes its stand,
Each blade of grass, a work so grand.
A tapestry of winter's charms,
Wrapped in nature's soothing arms.

With each step, a crunch of sound,
Fond memories in silence found.
Frosty breath hangs in the air,
A tranquil moment, always rare.

As day unfolds with gentle grace,
Luminous frost has left its trace.
Slumbering fields, forever bright,
In the soft embrace of morning light.

Veins of Ice in the Wilderness

Veins of ice in silent ground,
Whispers echo, nature's sound.
Frosted crystals, sunlight's gaze,
In the woods, where time decays.

Shadows dance on snow-capped hills,
Breezes carry winter's chills.
Nature's breath, a frozen sigh,
Underneath the cobalt sky.

Footsteps crunch, the world is stark,
Footprints lead to nature's arc.
In this realm, the cold holds sway,
A land where warmth has lost its way.

Silhouettes of trees emerge,
From the white, where ice will surge.
Veins of wilderness still pulse,
In this realm, where silence swells.

Battles fought beneath the frost,
Life persists, despite the cost.
In the echoes, history speaks,
Of survival in the peaks.

The Unraveled Tapestry of Chill

Frayed edges of the woven night,
Stars are scattered, cold and bright.
Fabrics woven with threads of gray,
Whispers of a long-lost day.

Patches sewn of dreams resigned,
In this chill, the heart confined.
Each breath pulled, a shaky sound,
Through the cold, where warmth is drowned.

Beneath the weight of silent skies,
The tapestry begins to rise.
Threads of silver drape the ground,
In the absence, life is found.

Colors fade in winter's breath,
Woven tales of love and death.
In the chill, community binds,
Seeking warmth that hope still finds.

The loom of life, it spins and sways,
Creating patterns, dark and grays.
In its grasp, the heart shall feel,
An unraveled tale, so surreal.

Cold Whispers Through the Pines

Cold whispers weave through ancient pines,
Telling tales of frost and lines.
Secrets linger, heavy air,
In this chill, the world is bare.

Branches shiver in the night,
Moonbeams cast a ghostly light.
Nature's voice, a soft exhale,
Guiding hearts along the trail.

Frozen moments, time shall freeze,
Rustling leaves in gentle breeze.
Echoes dance beneath the boughs,
Frost-kissed minstrels take their vows.

In the stillness, spirits play,
In this dreamlike, cold ballet.
Whispers breathe through tranquil trees,
Spreading warmth with every sneeze.

Stories told in quiet tones,
Amongst the roots, the heart atones.
Cold whispers, life's gentle song,
In the pines, where souls belong.

Caged Air of a Frozen Breath

Caged air held in frozen seams,
Dancing softly on moonlit beams.
Breath like ice and words subdued,
In the night, where life is brooded.

A world wrapped in silver lace,
Each heartbeat finds a softer pace.
Caged whispers echo through the still,
As shadows play on window sill.

With each gust, the world confined,
Breath and sound, intertwined.
Frosted panes reveal the night,
Invisible, yet filled with light.

Caged air swirls with visions clear,
Silent songs that we hold dear.
In the depths of winter's hold,
Stories rise, waiting to be told.

A moment captured in the gleam,
Within the caged, the spirit dreams.
Breath of winter, cold yet bright,
In its grasp, life takes flight.

The Resilience of Frozen Ferns

Beneath the frost, they stand so tall,
Green survivors, answering the call.
Still thriving midst the icy breath,
They whisper strength beyond all death.

Through crystal nights, their spirits gleam,
A silent tale, a frozen dream.
In delicate dance, they brave the cold,
A story of warmth, quietly told.

Each frosty leaf a testament bright,
Of lasting hope in the darkest night.
Beneath the snow, they hold their ground,
A wondrous peace in silence found.

Time will pass, the seasons sway,
These frozen ferns will find their way.
With sunlight's touch, they will arise,
And spread their wings toward the skies.

For in the heart where winter's bold,
Resilience blooms like tales of old.
The frozen ferns, with roots so deep,
In chilling grasp, their secrets keep.

A Tapestry Woven in Snowflakes

In silent dance, the snowflakes fall,
A tapestry, nature's gentle call.
Each unique flake, a story unfolds,
Crafted in silence, beauty beholds.

They blanket the earth in shimmering white,
A quiet comfort, a soft delight.
With every drift, a world reborn,
Morning's canvas, fresh with dawn.

Children laugh in the frosty air,
Snowball fights and winter's flair.
Footprints tracing in the snow,
A fleeting mark where memories grow.

As the sun sets, hues intertwine,
Orange and pink on white so fine.
A fleeting moment, a stolen glance,
Nature's stage, in winter's dance.

So let us cherish this snowy grace,
A fleeting masterpiece we embrace.
In every flake, a whispered tale,
A tapestry where dreams prevail.

The Fragility of a Winter's Heart

Beneath the ice, a beating soul,
In winter's grip, it longs to whole.
A fragile heart, encased in chill,
Yearning for warmth, a silent thrill.

The breath of frost on window panes,
Echoes of hopes and distant pains.
As long nights creep and shadows creep,
A tender wish begins to weep.

In the dim light, a flicker glows,
A promise made where the cold wind blows.
For every tear, a speck of dawn,
A fragile heart shall carry on.

Yet as the snow begins to melt,
A whisper of spring, the heart once felt.
In every thaw, soft blooms arise,
Reminders sent from winter's sighs.

Though fragile it seems in winter's clutch,
Hope still lingers with a gentle touch.
The heart shall mend, though cold may reign,
For love endures through joy and pain.

Guardian of the Crystal Woods

In a grove where silence reigns,
The crystal woods hold ancient chains.
Guardian tall, with branches wide,
Stands sentinel where dreams abide.

Each snow-kissed bough, a tale to tell,
Of whispered secrets and magic's spell.
In frosted light, their shadows dance,
A timeless moment, a fleeting glance.

Through winter's breath, they keep the night,
A steadfast guide, a beacon bright.
In hollowed trunks, the voices hum,
Of seasons passed and journeys come.

When twilight fades and stars ignite,
The guardian watches, a tranquil sight.
With every flake that graces the ground,
A promise of peace in stillness found.

Forever standing, strong and proud,
Embracing nature, shrouded in cloud.
The crystal woods and guardian dear,
A sacred space where hearts can steer.

Glimmering Paths in the Tempest

Through shadows deep, the lights will guide,
A whisper soft, where hopes reside.
With every storm, a path appears,
In darkened winds, we cast our fears.

When thunder roars, the heart takes flight,
With glimmering dreams, we chase the night.
Each raindrop sings a tale unknown,
In tempest's hold, we find our own.

The earth might tremble, the skies may cry,
But within our souls, the stars still lie.
With every step, we break the chains,
To find our truth beneath the rains.

So let the storm rage wild and free,
We'll dance together, you and me.
Amid the chaos, hand in hand,
We'll weave our dreams into the land.

Through glimmering paths, we forge our fate,
For love will guide us, never late.
In every tempest, we shall thrive,
Embracing storms, we come alive.

The Shiver of Dreams

In quiet corners, shadows play,
A shiver speaks what words can't say.
Upon the canvas of the night,
Dreams take flight in silver light.

Whispers linger, soft and low,
As dusk unfolds its velvet glow.
Each sigh transforms the air we breathe,
In dreams, we find what hearts believe.

The moonlight dances on the skin,
Awakening the thoughts within.
As dreams unravel, time stands still,
Embracing hope, the heart's sweet thrill.

In waking hours, we chase the dawn,
Yet in these dreams, our fears are gone.
With every flicker, visions grow,
The shiver lingers, soft and slow.

So let us wander, brave and free,
In the realm of dreams, just you and me.
Where every heartbeat, pure and true,
Is woven deep in moments new.

Midnight's Blanket of Silence

The clock strikes twelve, the world holds breath,
In midnight's grasp, we find our heft.
A blanket soft, so still, serene,
Envelops dreams in twilight's sheen.

The stars above, like stories told,
In silence deep, their light unfolds.
In quietude, our secrets weave,
A tapestry of what we believe.

With every heartbeat, whispers flow,
In hush profound, the feelings grow.
As shadows dance along the wall,
In midnight's grip, we hear the call.

The moonlight drapes a silver veil,
In echoes soft, our hearts set sail.
Through silent hours, love's song remains,
In midnight's hush, our joy sustains.

So let us linger, lost in time,
Within this realm, where dreams chime.
In midnight's weight, we find our light,
Within the silence, hearts take flight.

Elysium Wrapped in Frost

In winter's breath, a world divine,
Elysium glows in silver line.
With frosted petals, dreams unfold,
A paradise, a tale retold.

The air is crisp, like whispered vows,
As nature dons her white-tipped gowns.
Each flake a note, a gentle song,
In frozen realms, where we belong.

The trees stand tall, like guardians wise,
Beneath the weight of azure skies.
In frosty stillness, spirits soar,
Elysium's charm, forevermore.

With every breath, we taste the chill,
Yet warmth within does linger still.
In moments shared, the heart finds rest,
This frozen land, our sacred quest.

Together we roam, hand in hand,
In Elysium's glow, a timeless land.
Wrapped in frost, our dreams ignite,
In winter's arms, our hearts take flight.

Midnight's Shimmering Layer

Stars twinkle softly in the night,
A canvas of dreams in silver light.
Whispers of secrets softly sway,
In the shimmering dawn, shadows play.

The moon bathes earth in tranquil glow,
A layer of magic lying low.
Silver dust dances through the breeze,
Kisses the night, as spirits tease.

With every twinkle, hearts ignite,
Lost in the beauty, pure delight.
Time stands still in this twilight,
Wrapped in peace, 'tween day and night.

Echoes of laughter fill the air,
Moments like this, beyond compare.
Into the dreams, we gently glide,
On satin sheets where wishes bide.

A final bow as dawn draws near,
The shimmering layer disappears.
Yet in our souls, the memories stay,
A midnight kiss that won't decay.

Enchanted by the Winter's Touch

Snowflakes dance like fleeting dreams,
Blanketing earth in silver seams.
Whispers of winter, crisp and clear,
Bring forth magic that draws us near.

Branches glisten with frosty lace,
Nature's art, a gentle embrace.
Footprints linger in the dusky white,
Stories woven through starry night.

The world around is serene and still,
Hearts are warmed by winter's thrill.
A crackling fire, a cozy space,
Love wrapped in winter's soft embrace.

Underneath the glittering sky,
Frosted whispers will never die.
Enchanting sights that soothe the soul,
In winter's charm, we are made whole.

A soft reminder of beauty's clutch,
Captured sweetly in winter's touch.
As the seasons change, we'll always hold,
These moments shared, worth more than gold.

Eclipsed by Shards of Ice

Beneath a veil of glimmering frost,
A world transformed, beauty embossed.
Shards of ice like crystal dreams,
Glitter and shine in moonlit beams.

Glistening branches bow and bend,
Nature's art that knows no end.
In the silence, secrets freeze,
As the heart learns to trust the ease.

Time stands still in this frozen trance,
Life's fleeting moments softly dance.
Eclipsed by wonder, we remain,
In the beauty, joy, and pain.

The air is crisp with magic's sigh,
Under the expansive, starry sky.
Each shard reflects our deepest fears,
And holds the whispers of our tears.

Yet in this chill, hope flickers bright,
A promise born from darkest night.
Eclipsed but not lost, love will rise,
Beyond the shards, see through new eyes.

Heartbeats in the Frozen Grove

In the grove where silence reigns,
Nature's heartbeat flows through veins.
Trees like guardians, strong and tall,
Whisper the secrets of it all.

Frozen leaves beneath our feet,
Echoes of life in the bittersweet.
In the cold, our laughter flares,
Warming the air, shaking the cares.

Each heartbeat speaks of stories shared,
Memories woven, hearts laid bare.
Through the frost, new dreams will bloom,
In the shadows of winter's gloom.

The sun dips low, painting the night,
Hearts aglow in fading light.
Together we stand, hand in hand,
In the frozen grove, we understand.

Embraced by winter's tender grace,
We find our rhythm, our own place.
Through every heartbeat, love will flow,
In this enchanted, frozen grove.

Echoes in the Icebound Forest

Whispers wander through the trees,
A silence drapes, crisp with ease.
Footsteps soft on frostbound ground,
In this stillness, peace is found.

Branches bare, a pale embrace,
Nature holds a frozen grace.
Echoes linger, time stands still,
In the heart of winter's chill.

Moonlight spills like silver thread,
Guiding paths where few have tread.
A world cocooned in quiet white,
Dreams take flight in the night.

Softly falls the gentle snow,
In its hush, wild wonders grow.
Every flake, a tale untold,
In the forest, brave and bold.

Nature sings a lullaby,
As the stars blink in the sky.
Echoes fade, yet still remain,
In the icebound, sweet refrain.

Shadows of the Frosted Moon

Underneath a silver glow,
Shadows dance, moving slow.
Nighttime whispers secrets deep,
In the stillness, dreams we keep.

Frosted beams on glistening leaves,
Nature weaves what heart believes.
A tapestry of night and light,
Guiding souls in soft twilight.

Whispers echo in the dark,
Each soft sound a fleeting spark.
The moon hangs low, a watchful eye,
Drawing forth the nightingale's sigh.

Stars emerge, a scattered trail,
In this magic, we set sail.
Through the shadows, shadows weave,
In their dance, we dare believe.

Endless wonder fills the night,
Wrapped in warmth, a pure delight.
Shadows fall but never fade,
With the frost, dreams are made.

The Quiet Dance of Snowflakes

Falling soft from skies above,
Snowflakes twirl, a dance of love.
Each unique in form and grace,
They find their home, a perfect space.

Whispers swirl as currents blow,
A gentle hush within the snow.
Silent ballet in the air,
Enchanting beauty everywhere.

Wrapped in white, the earth does sigh,
As snowflakes kiss the world good-bye.
With every flutter, they compose,
A symphony of winter's prose.

In the glow of muted light,
They embrace the tranquil night.
Dancing dreams of winter's song,
In the stillness, we belong.

Softly they lay, a quilted seam,
Crafted from a snowflakes' dream.
In their grace, we find a chance,
To join in winter's quiet dance.

Time Suspended in Crystal

Frozen moments, crystal clear,
In the stillness, time draws near.
A snapshot caught in winter's breath,
Life continues, even in death.

Icicles hang, suspended bright,
Each a story, veiled in light.
Twinkles of the season's art,
Chilling whispers touch the heart.

Frozen landscapes, quiet, bold,
Tales of time yet to be told.
Every flake, a fleeting quest,
In their beauty, we find rest.

Moments linger, taste of frost,
In this space, we fear no loss.
Time is patient, time will bend,
In crystal silence, we ascend.

Underneath the frozen skies,
Life embraces, never dies.
In the stillness, dreams ignite,
Suspended time, a pure delight.

Fragments of a Frozen Mirage

In the stillness, whispers cling,
Icicles hang, a crystal ring.
Mirages dance in frigid light,
Echoes blend with fading night.

Footprints carved in powdered snow,
Stories told in winter's glow.
Frozen breaths in silver threads,
Memories crawl where silence treads.

Mountains wearing cloaks of white,
Veils that hide the day from sight.
Nature's canvas, pure and bright,
Artistry in cold's delight.

Shadows flit where breezes flow,
Caught in time, yet never slow.
Each fragment speaks, a tale unsaid,
Of all the dreams that winter bred.

Silent thoughts in frozen streams,
Beneath the ice, the world redeems.
In mirage, we find our peace,
As fleeting moments softly cease.

Frosted Lullabies Under Starry Skies

Hold me close with winter's song,
Where dreams and starlight both belong.
Frosted whispers, soft and sweet,
Cradle hearts in rhythmic beat.

Night unfolds with snowy veils,
Dancing lightly, swirling trails.
Each note lingers, gently spun,
In the hush where day is done.

Stars glitter in the quiet air,
Frosted wishes everywhere.
Lullabies of night embrace,
While soft flakes drift through space.

Ethereal scents of pine and snow,
Guide our spirits high and low.
Underneath celestial fires,
Hope resides in soft desires.

So let the world drift into dreams,
As moonlight dances on the streams.
Frosted lullabies fill the night,
Cocooned in silver, pure delight.

Shivers of the Silent Moon

Moonlight tints the world in gray,
Whispers echo oceans away.
Shivers dance on winter's breath,
Carrying tales of life and death.

Silhouettes in quiet grace,
Each shadow finds its lonely place.
The moon, a watchful, silent guide,
Casts her glow, though worlds may hide.

Snowflakes shimmer, softly fall,
An embrace that blankets all.
In the stillness, hearts will shiver,
Tracing paths along the river.

Cold embraces, yet so warm,
Nature's peace, a calming charm.
Beneath the moon's profound decree,
Silent dreams are born to be.

Stillness stirs the depths of night,
As shadows dance in silver light.
Shivers wrapped around the moon,
Sing a haunting, tranquil tune.

When Nature Holds Its Breath

A moment caught in still repose,
Nature pauses, time bestows.
Every leaf and branch now still,
Whispers float, a tranquil thrill.

Clouds hang still in endless gray,
As if waiting for the day.
Breezes soft, no rustling leaves,
Every heart in silence weaves.

Frozen rivers lose their flow,
In this peace, the world will grow.
Snowflakes swirl in artful flight,
Painting landscapes pure and bright.

Frozen echoes fill the air,
Nature's breath, a sacred prayer.
When time pauses, and stillness thrives,
Magic seeps where silence dives.

A shiver hangs, and then it's gone,
Yet in the quiet, life goes on.
When nature sleeps, it knows its worth,
In gentle dreams of quiet earth.

Symphony of the Silvered Trees

Beneath the sky so wide and clear,
The silvered trees whisper near.
Their branches sway in gentle grace,
A symphony of nature's embrace.

With leaves that twinkle in the sun,
Their dance continues, never done.
A melody that soothes the soul,
In harmony, they make us whole.

The breezes carry sweet refrains,
A song that lives beyond the plains.
Each note a whisper, soft and true,
In every moment, life anew.

As twilight casts its golden glow,
The symphony begins to flow.
The night unfolds with stars so bright,
While silver trees hold dreams in sight.

In every branch and every leaf,
Resides the magic, pure belief.
In silent nights or sunny days,
The silvered trees share nature's ways.

Glistening Memories of the Past

In the mirror of time's embrace,
Glistening memories find their place.
Fleeting shadows, whispers sweet,
Echoes of moments, bittersweet.

Old photographs with edges torn,
Of laughter shared and hearts reborn.
They shimmer like dew at dawn,
A fleeting glimpse before they're gone.

The stories told in twilight's glow,
Of loves we held and dreams aglow.
Each tale a thread, a vibrant hue,
Woven deep in all we do.

Through the winds of change we drift,
Carried along, memories gift.
In every smile, a tale unfolds,
Glistening treasures, love retold.

So cherish each echo, soft and clear,
In glistening memories, hold them near.
For in the heart, they ever last,
A timeless bond with the past.

Whirlwind of Frost and Dreams

In the quiet hush of winter's breath,
A whirlwind spins, a dance with death.
Frosty whispers call the night,
As dreams take flight in silver light.

The world adorned in icy lace,
Ghostly figures softly trace.
Through the chill, a pulse of warmth,
In dreams, we find our hearts reborn.

With every flake that gently falls,
A tale of hope, the spirit calls.
In swirling drifts, the visions bloom,
A garden dressed in winter's gloom.

As midnight strikes, the stars ignite,
Guided by their shimmering light.
The whirlwind whirls both fierce and free,
In swirling ardor, a reverie.

Amidst the frost, we dare to dream,
With hearts entwined in silver beams.
The whirlwind sings, a timeless song,
In every pulse, we all belong.

Silent Laughter of the Crystal Winds

In the stillness of the night so deep,
Gentle whispers, secrets keep.
The crystal winds, they softly play,
With laughter echoing through the gray.

Each breeze a touch, a tender sigh,
Inviting dreams to soar and fly.
Among the branches, a playful sound,
Silent laughter where love is found.

With every gust, the world awakes,
In the calm, a promise makes.
The dance of leaves, a quiet tune,
Reminding us of stars and moon.

Through twilight's veil, the shadows blend,
Crystal winds, our loyal friends.
In the night, their laughter flows,
A symphony that ever grows.

So let us listen, hearts aligned,
To the whispers of the kind.
In silent laughter, we'll embrace,
The crystal winds, our sacred space.

The Stillness of Crystal Nights

Stars shimmer bright in the dark sky,
Whispers of silence, a gentle sigh.
Moonlight dances on the frozen ground,
In this stillness, peace can be found.

Winds softly caress the barren trees,
Carrying secrets on the night breeze.
Dreams unfold in the velvet glow,
Wrapped in magic, we feel the flow.

Each breath lingers in the crisp air,
A moment cherished without a care.
Frosted branches glimmer in light,
Nature's beauty, a wondrous sight.

Time stands still in this frozen land,
Embraced by winter's gentle hand.
Hearts find solace in crystal nights,
In this stillness, the soul ignites.

Echoes of Cold Serenity

A tranquil hush envelops the ground,
In the frosty air, peace can be found.
Footsteps echo on the icy path,
Whispers of calm in winter's breath.

Snowflakes twirl like dreams in flight,
Glistening softly in pale moonlight.
The world is hushed beneath a white veil,
Nature's whispers tell a silent tale.

Frozen lakes reflect the starry dome,
In this quiet space, we feel at home.
Stillness surrounds like a soft embrace,
Creating a haven, a sacred place.

Branches bow low with crystal weight,
Each frozen droplet a sacred fate.
Ethereal stillness rests in the air,
In echoes of cold, we find our prayer.

Serenity reigns in frosted bliss,
Each moment savored is one not to miss.
In winter's grasp, our hearts align,
Finding solace in the divine.

Frost-kissed Memories of Yesterday

Whispers trace back to days gone by,
Frost-kissed moments, they never die.
Laughter echoes through the crisp air,
Memories linger, tender and rare.

Shadows dance in the pale moon's light,
Painting the past, a beautiful sight.
Each flake that falls tells a story true,
Of joy and warmth in the cold, anew.

Sprigs of pine hold the scent of time,
Frosted memories wrapped in rhyme.
A flicker of warmth amidst the chill,
Reminders of love, a gentle thrill.

With every breath, nostalgia flows,
As winter's chill on the heart grows.
In the stillness of this crystal night,
Frost-kissed memories feel so right.

Embracing the past, we find our way,
In the gentle hush of another day.
Timeless treasures, forever to stay,
Frost-kissed memories won't fade away.

Shadows Beneath Gleaming White

Beneath the blanket of purest white,
Shadows whisper in the soft twilight.
Tracks of wanderers left behind,
In every step, a story entwined.

Frosty whispers dance on the breeze,
Rustling the branches of ancient trees.
Each shadowy corner holds a tale,
Of winter's magic, ever frail.

The stillness cradles the world around,
In the silence, deeper truths are found.
Glistening frost paints a world anew,
Where memories linger, fragile yet true.

Warm hearts gather in the chilling night,
Sharing stories 'til morning light.
Shadows beneath gleaming white show,
The warmth within despite the snow.

In the quiet glow, we find our way,
With shadows guiding us, come what may.
In gleaming white, our spirits soar,
Embracing winter's beauty evermore.

www.ingramcontent.com/pod-product-compliance
Ingram Content Group UK Ltd.
Pitfield, Milton Keynes, MK11 3LW, UK
UKHW031944151224
452382UK00006B/133